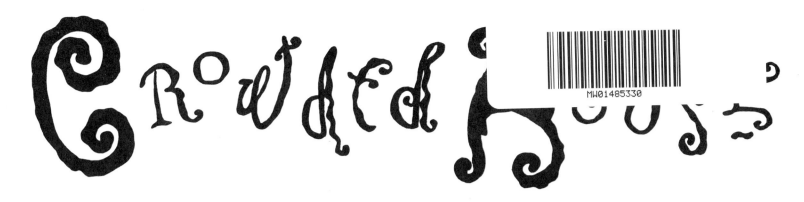

CONTENTS

Piano/Vocal Arrangements by Donald Sosin, Alan Rosenthal and
   Mark Phillips
Associate Music Editor: Mark Phillips
Art Direction: Alisa Hill
Production Manager: Daniel Rosenbaum
Administration: Deborah Poletto

ISBN: 0-89524-401-2

BETTER BE HOME SOON

Words and Music by
Neil Finn

soon. _____ Oh. ____ That's why I tell ___ you, ____

you'd bet-ter be home ___ soon.

molto rit.

I FEEL POSSESSED

Words and Music by
Neil Finn

ex - pla - na - tion. I'm not ly - in', _____ not ask - in' for an-

y - thing. _____ I just want to be ___ there when it hap - pens a - gain.

___ I hard - ly know ___ which way is up ___ or which ___ way down. _____

___ Peo - ple are strange, ___ God on - ly knows. _____ I feel pos - sessed _____

when you_ come 'round.

When-ev - er you in - vade my home,_ ev - 'ry- thing I know_ flies

I feel pos-sessed ___ when you ___ come 'round. ___

I feel pos-sessed. ___

I feel pos-sessed. ___

I feel pos-sessed. ___

molto rit.

11

INTO TEMPTATION

Words and Music by
Neil Finn

The guilt-y get _ no sleep in the last _ slow hours _ of morn - ing. _ Ex - pe - ri - ence is cheap. _ I should have lis - tened to _ the warn - ing. _ But the cra - dle is soft _ and warm! _ In - to temp-ta - tion, know - in' full well _ the earth

LOVE THIS LIFE

Words and Music by
Neil Finn

IN THE LOWLANDS

Words and Music by
Neil Finn

2nd time skip to Chorus

The first drops land on the win-dow, the first sign that there's some-thing wrong.

Play 1st time only

Light rain and a head full of thun-der, Which way? Which way?

Two days till I get to you.

I'll be late if I ev-

Additional Lyrics

2. The sky fell underneath a blanket.
   The sun sank as the miles went by.
   Sit back with your head on the pillow.
   When you remember it makes you cry.
   Ghost cars on the freeway
   Like friends that you thought you had.
   One by one they are disappearing. *(To Chorus)*

SISTER MADLY

Words and Music by
Neil Finn

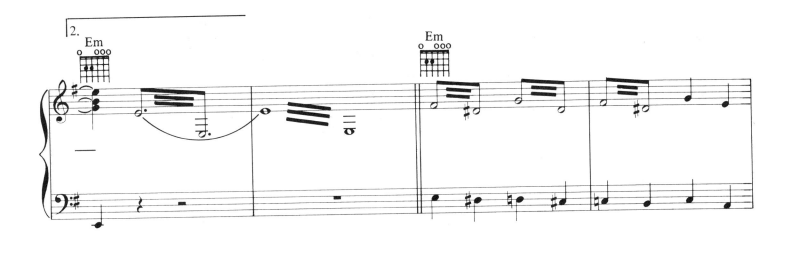

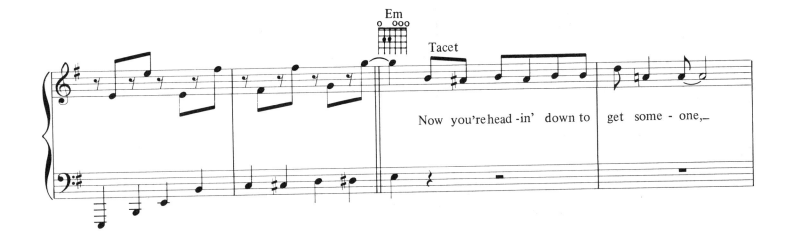

Now you're head -in' down to get some - one,—

some-one— that you should - 've had years a - go.— The po - si - tion is

com - in' through.___ All the peo -ple that you're stand - ing on.___

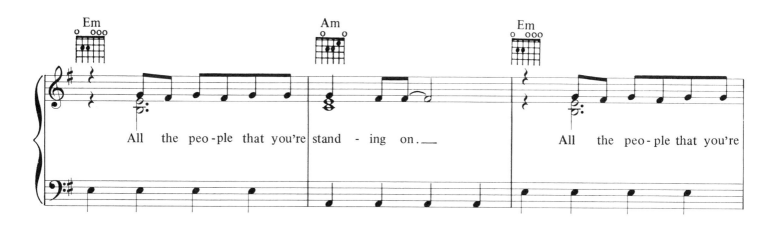

All   the peo -ple that you're stand - ing   on.___   All   the peo -ple that you're

stand - ing on.___   You're hard to get a hand on.   Sis - ter

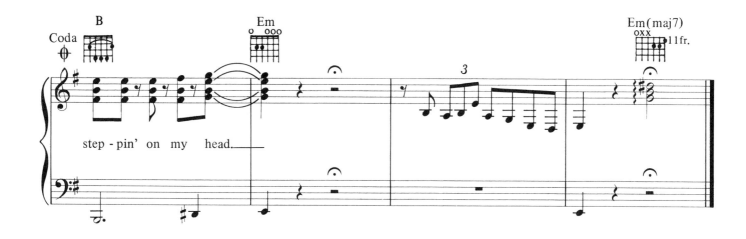

step -pin' on my head.___

KILL EYE

Words and Music by
Neil Finn

Kill eye,_____ half - way to hell and be - yond._

WHEN YOU COME

Words and Music by
Neil Finn

MANSION IN THE SLUMS

Words and Music by
Neil Finn

*Pianists: Omit high vocal line.

NEVER BE THE SAME

Words and Music by
Neil Finn

BRINGING ON THE HITS

CHERRY LANE MUSIC PRESENTS THE MUSIC OF TODAY'S HOTTEST STARS

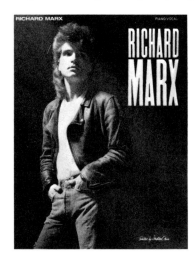

RICHARD MARX

All the songs from the smash debut album by singer/songwriter Richard Marx. Features the hit singles "Don't Mean Nothing," "Should've Known Better" and "Endless Summer Nights." Plus full color fold-out and complete lyrics.
#7911

NEW!

Bruce Hornsby And The Range
SCENES FROM THE SOUTHSIDE

Matching folio to the second hit album from Grammy Award winner Bruce Hornsby and The Range. Includes the smash single "The Valley Road" and nine more sensational songs all featuring Bruce Hornsby's piano solos. Plus photos and complete lyrics.
#5313

NOW AVAILABLE
THE MUSIC OF BRUCE HORNSBY
FOR EASY PIANO

All the songs from the double-platinum debut album "The Way It Is" plus "Jacob's Ladder." This great collection of songs for easy piano includes interviews, photos and background on the songs.
#5308

NEW!

Rick Springfield
ROCK OF LIFE

"Rock of Life," "Honeymoon in Beirut" and all the songs from Rick Springfield's sixth hit album are featured in this terrific matching folio. A great collection! Photos and complete lyrics included.
#7923

HENRY LEE SUMMER

Matching folio to the super-charged album features the hit singles "I Wish I Had A Girl," "Darlin' Danielle Don't" and eight other great songs. Plus full color fold-out, complete lyrics and background on one of the year's hottest new stars.
#7924

Cherry
Lane Music
Company, Inc.
"quality in printed music"
P.O. Box 430, Port Chester, NY 10573-430